To A
Lul
Alacovie.

With special thanks
To Martin Kerr and Amy Schneider for beautiful book design.
To Helen Exley for believing in my work and your constant wise
counsel throughout this project.
To my husband Jim, for everything.

Published in 2002 by Exley Publications Ltd in Great Britain.
16 Chalk Hill, Watford, Herts WD19 4BG, UK
Published in 2003 by Exley Publications LLC in the USA.
185 Main Street, Spencer, MA 01562, USA
www.helenexleygiftbooks.com
12 11 10 9 8 7 6 5 4 3
Copyright © Susan Squellati Florence 2002.
The moral right of the author has been asserted.
ISBN 1-86187-417-0

Edited by Helen Exley. Printed in China.
Written and illustrated by Susan Squellati Florence

Helen Exley Giftbooks cover the most powerful of all human
relationships: love between couples, the bonds within families and
between friends. No expense is spared in making sure that each book
is as thoughtful and meaningful a gift as it is possible to create: good
to give, good to receive. You have the result in your hands. If you
have loved it — tell others! We'd rather put the money into more good
books than spend it on advertising. There is no power on earth like
the word-of-mouth recommendation of friends.

YOUR JOURNEY

A passage through a difficult time

WRITTEN & ILLUSTRATED BY

Susan Squellati Florence

A HELEN EXLEY GIFTBOOK

Most of us will journey through painful life passages. It may be a time of deep loss or serious illness. It may be a time of facing problems in a relationship or feeling the pain of an addiction and seeking help. It may be that something within ourself is changing and that we are afraid.

It takes courage to answer the calling of these times of trial. It takes strength to enter the sacred place of our soul. We will be humble and vulnerable in this time of unknowing.

These painful passages allow the metal of who we are to be transformed into who we are becoming. In the unknowing, we can receive wisdom. In the darkness there is light to help us see things differently. We can endure what life has put in our path and grow spiritually because of it.

I hope this book will give you strength on your journey. I hope this book will help bring acceptance of this unknowing time and understanding in opening up to the pain and unbearable sadness that are part of our being human.

There is a place of peace awaiting us all. I hope **Your Journey** will be a help as you find this peace within yourself.

There is a journey
awaiting you.

It comes in truth
and promise...

when you reach the point
of not knowing
who you are...
and have no place to go.

*This most precious
and painful passage
is the journey
to yourself.*

You will

travel to places

never visited before,

where you meet

unspoken fears,

and unearth

buried truths.

You will climb

high and perilous mountains,

those that rise up

from inside yourself.

You will explore

forgotten waters

held deep

in the sea

of your soul.

You will be stranded
in the wilderness,
and find a way
through pathless land.

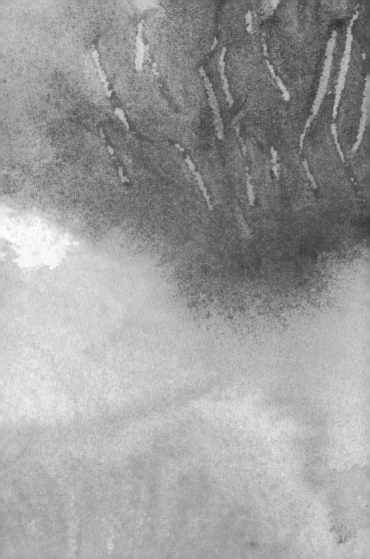

You will learn

to walk slowly...

step

by

step.

It will be impossible

to see beyond

what is in front of you.

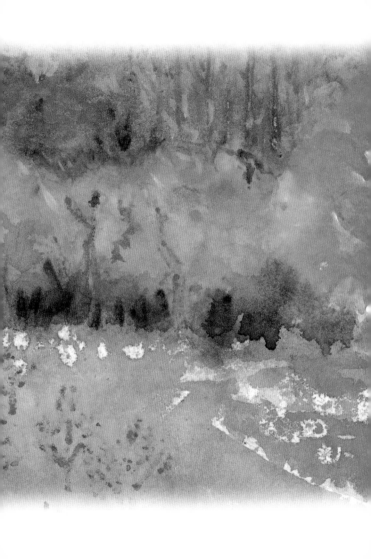

You will be lost

before you are found.

You will be empty

before you are full.

You will cry

the deep sobs of the earth

and tears of rain

will cleanse the house

around your heart.

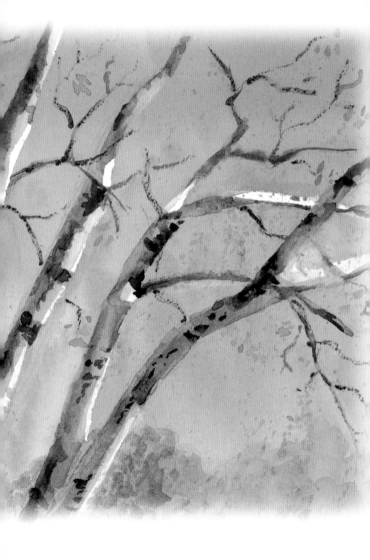

In time,

like spring

coming

to the bare

branches

of winter's

tree...

*...you will begin
your own new growth.*

In time,

like shafts of light

streaming down

into the forest...

you will see
your way through.

In time,
*   because life,*
like birth and death,
*   knows its own time...*

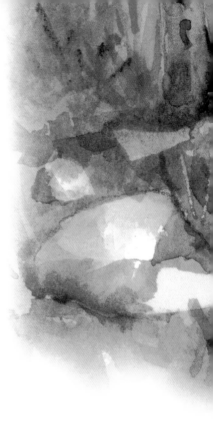

your
fears
and
struggles
and
unknowing
will be
transformed.

Your heart

will become open

to unchartered landscapes

as you travel through life.

your heart

will become open

Your soul

will become

a reflecting pool

whose crystal clear waters

reveal your own

deep mysteries.

You will understand
why the wave crashes to the shore
then returns to the deep
for new momentum.

DERSTAND

The wings
of the butterfly
will be yours,

as you follow
the currents
of your heart's desires.

The work of the honeybee

will be yours,

as you seek sweet nectar

for your daily life.

The flight of the eagle

will be yours

as your spirit soars

to high lofty places.

You will
become one
with who you really are.

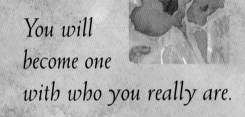

Your life

will hold truth,

promise and meaning.

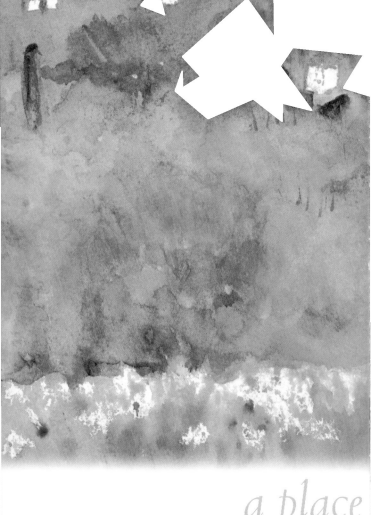

a place

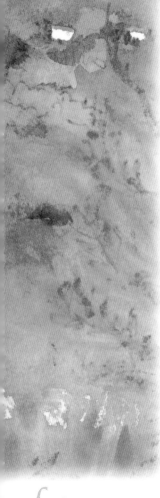

At journey's end
you will find
a place of peace
within yourself.

of peace

Susan Squellati Florence

The well loved and collected greeting cards of Susan Florence
have sold hundreds of millions of copies in the last
three decades. Her giftbooks have sold over one and a half
million copies.

With words of gentle wisdom and original paintings, Susan
Florence brings her unique style to all her gift products and
her readers have written time and again to thank her and tell
her how the books were a profound help to them. People have
told Susan that her words speak to them of what they cannot
say... but what they feel.

Susan Florence's completely new collection of giftbooks in
The Journeys Series invites the readers to pause and look
deeply into their lives. "We all need more time to rediscover
and reflect on what is meaningful and important in our own

lives... and what brings us joy and beauty. Writing these books in The Journeys Series has helped me understand more fully the value of love and acceptance in helping us through the difficult times as we journey through life."

Susan lives with her husband, Jim, in Ojai, California. They have two grown children, Brent and Emily.

THE JOURNEYS SERIES

1-86187-420-0
Change... *is a place where new journeys begin*

1-86187-422-7
How wonderful it is... **Having Friends in Our Lives**

1-86187-418-9
On the Gift of A Mother's Love
For my mother from your daughter a mother too

1-86187-419-7
Take Time Alone *The gift of being with yourself*

1-86187-421-9
When You Lose Someone You Love
...a journey through the heart of grief

1-86187-417-0
Your Journey
...a passage through a difficult time